EL POTRERO CHICO
ROCK CLIMBING
2024

Hiking, Climbing, and Beyond in Hidalgo, Mexico

Copyright © 2024 by Hans Markûsson

All rights reserved. No part of this book may be reproduced, stored in a retrieval system, or transmitted in any form or by any means, electronic, mechanical, photocopying, recording, scanning, or otherwise, without the prior written permission of the publisher, except for brief quotations embodied in critical reviews and certain other non-commercial uses permitted by copyright law.

Disclaimer

This Guide book offers information and insights based on the author's research and experiences. While every effort has been made for accuracy, the author and publisher disclaim any liability for the use or application of the content. Readers are encouraged to exercise discretion, seek professional advice, and acknowledge that personal outcomes may vary. The views expressed are those of the author and not necessarily endorsed by any mentioned organization or individual. By using this book, readers accept these terms and take full responsibility for any actions they undertake based on the information provided.

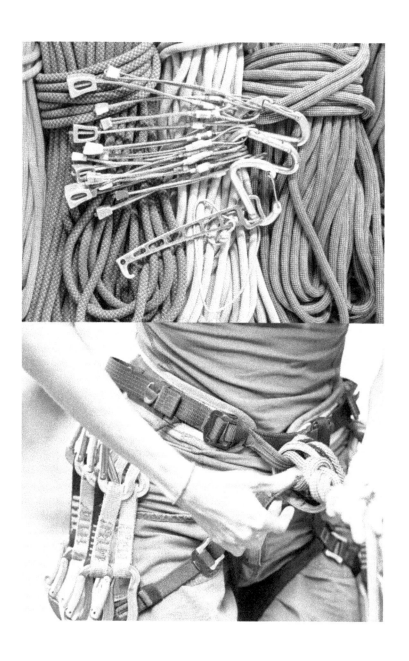

INTRODUCTION.. 9

Chapter 1: El Potrero Chico - A Climber's Paradise Beckons. 13

1.1: A Tapestry of History and Rock. 14

1.2: A Geography Forged for Climbers. 14

1.3: When to Dance with the Limestone. 14

1.4: Getting to El Potrero Chico. 15

1.5 Accommodation and Amenities: Campsites, Hotels, and Restaurants 17

Chapter 2: Gearing Up for Success - Conquering Limestone with Confidence 21

2.1: Packing Smart - Your Climbing Arsenal 21

2.2: Footwork Finesse - Choosing the Right Footwear. 23

2.3: Layering Up for Limestone Adventures. 24

2.4: Gearing Up for Multi-Pitch Adventures - Conquering Multi-Legged Giants 25

2.5: Climbing Etiquette and Leave No Trace Principles. 26

Chapter 3: The Crags of El Potrero Chico. 32

Chapter 4: Mastering the Climb - Unveiling the Secrets of Limestone Ascension 46

Chapter 5: Beyond the Climb - Embracing the Full El Potrero Chico Experience 56

Appendix: Climbing El Potrero Chico with Confidence. 62

A. Deepening Your Journey - Resources and Further Information 62

B. Conversion Tables. 64

C. Sample Packing List for El Potrero Chico: 65

Bonus Section. 68

6.1: Glossary of Climbing Terms. 68

6.2: Useful Phrases and Numbers with Pronunciation Guide (Spanish - English): 72

6.3 Downloadable Maps and Recommended Climbing Areas 76

Beyond the Climb: 10 Must-Do Activities. 78

INTRODUCTION

Dust motes danced in the golden light filtering through the canyon walls, swirling around my belay stance like miniature climbers scaling invisible air. Above, my partner, a blur of focused movement, fought his way up the blank face of "Taj Mahal." The rhythmic click of his carabiners echoed in the vast amphitheater of El Potrero Chico, a symphony composed of limestone, sweat, and ambition.

Twenty years ago, I first tasted the bitter-sweet magic of this place. I was a wide-eyed newbie, clinging to overhangs with trembling fingers, mesmerized by the towering walls that promised endless challenges. Time has sculpted my hands, etching calluses like topographic maps of countless ascents. My gaze sweeps across the sprawling amphitheater, recognizing routes like old friends: "Arathana," a slender thread of beauty weaving skyward; "Chinaco," a brutal test of endurance; "Aztlán," a multi-pitch masterpiece etched into the heart of the canyon.

There's a reverence in the air here, a respect for the history etched in the limestone. Whispers of Wolfgang Güllich,

Kurt Smith, and Beth Rodden echo through the crags, their daring ascents pushing the boundaries of human possibility. But El Potrero Chico isn't just for legends. It's a crucible for every climber, from wide-eyed beginners to grizzled veterans. Whether you're struggling up a 5.7 slab or clipping bolts on a 5.14c monster, the limestone whispers the same invitation: test your limits, push your fears, and discover the strength you never knew you possessed.

I clip in, the familiar tug of rope grounding me as I start my ascent. My fingers find the perfect edge, sending a familiar buzz through my forearms. This dance, this intimate communion with rock and sky, is a language I speak fluently. Below, the valley floor shrinks, transformed into a tapestry of vibrant greens and ochre browns. Time melts away, replaced by the singular focus of movement, breath, and the silent roar of ambition.

El Potrero Chico is more than just a climbing destination. It's a community, a melting pot of cultures and languages united by a shared passion. As I reach the top, breathless and exhilarated, I find myself surrounded by strangers who become instant friends, sharing stories around a crackling campfire under a sky dusted with a million stars. In their eyes, I see the same reflection of that first-time awe, the spark that I carry even after all these years.

Because El Potrero Chico isn't just about conquering routes; it's about conquering yourself. It's about stripping away the layers of doubt and fear, finding the strength to rise above your limitations, both physical and mental. It's about the raw joy of connecting with nature, with community, and with the best version of yourself. And that, my friends, is a climb worth taking, over and over again.

My Check

DATE _____

TOP 3 THINGS I LEARNT
_____
_____
_____

WHAT I AM WILLING TO TRY

THIS WEEK I FELT
_____

NEXT THING I WANT TO
_____
_____
_____

THINGS I ACCOMPLISHED THIS WEEK

WHAT WAS THE BEST THING ABOUT THE WEEK?

RATING
☆ ☆ ☆ ☆ ☆

El Potrero Chico

Chapter 1: El Potrero Chico - A Climber's Paradise Beckons

Prepare to have your expectations shattered and your climbing ambitions reignited. Nestled in the heart of Mexico's Nuevo León state, El Potrero Chico isn't just any climbing destination; it's a mecca, a coliseum of limestone etched with over 600 sport routes, each begging to be explored.

1.1: A Tapestry of History and Rock

El Potrero Chico's legacy stretches back millennia. Imagine ancient Teotihuacan traders traversing these very canyons, leaving whispers of their journey etched in the rock. Fast forward to the 1970s, when visionary German climber Kurt Albert discovered its potential and established the first routes. Since then, Potrero Chico has become a crucible for climbing legends like Wolfgang Güllich and Beth Rodden, each leaving their mark on this vertical tapestry.

1.2: A Geography Forged for Climbers

Imagine a dramatic amphitheater carved by eons of wind and water, its walls rising sheer and proud, a symphony of limestone textures sculpted in sun and shadow. That's El Potrero Chico. Towering over the quaint town of Hidalgo, this behemoth boasts over 20 distinct climbing sectors, each offering a unique playground. From the technical face climbs of Peñaflor to the endurance tests of El Toro, Potrero Chico caters to every climbing style and ambition.

1.3: When to Dance with the Limestone

Climate here is key. Aim for the "shoulder seasons" – November to March and September to October, when temperatures hover in the delightful 70s (Fahrenheit). Escape the summer heat (May to August), when temperatures can soar. Remember, winter nights (December to February) can get nippy, so pack some insulating layers.

Pro Tip: Mornings are golden! The sun paints the walls with a luminous warmth, perfect for sending those challenging projects. For afternoon shade, head to the south-facing sectors like La Silla or El Abra.

1.4: Getting to El Potrero Chico

Hidalgo, Nuevo León, Mexico – that's where you'll find this climber's haven. It's just a one-hour drive from the bustling city of Monterrey, making it easily accessible. Look for "El Potrero Chico National Park" on a map – that's where the magic begins.

With your climbing spirit ignited, let's navigate the logistics of reaching this limestone dreamland. Buckle up, adventurers, as we explore transportation options and navigate the charming town of Hidalgo.

Airborne Assault:

- Monterrey International Airport (MTY): Your aerial gateway to El Potrero Chico. Taxis and shuttles will whisk you to Hidalgo for $30-50 USD. Pre-booking is helpful, especially during peak season.
- Chartering Freedom: Feeling adventurous? Private planes can connect you directly to Hidalgo's airstrip, cutting travel time considerably. Prepare for a sky-high price tag, though.

Landbound Legions:

- ADO Bus: Embark on a comfortable journey from Monterrey on the ADO bus service. Tickets cost around $15-20 USD, and the ride offers a taste of Mexican landscapes.
- Motorized Manoeuvres: For independence and flexibility, rent a car in Monterrey. The drive takes about an hour, offering stunning canyon views.
- Parking at El Potrero Chico is ample, but fees apply. Consider carpooling to share the cost and the adventure.

Transportation Options and Costs:

- Flying: Monterrey's International Airport (MTY) is your gateway. Taxis or shuttles can whisk you to Hidalgo for around $30-50 USD.
- Bus: Take a comfortable ADO bus from Monterrey for around $15-20 USD.
- Driving: Rent a car or join a carpool from Monterrey. The drive is scenic, and parking is ample (though fees apply).

Distance from Key Locations:

- Monterrey: 50 km (31 miles)
- Saltillo: 180 km (112 miles)
- Ciudad Victoria: 300 km (186 miles)

1.5 Accommodation and Amenities: Campsites, Hotels, and Restaurants

Camping under the Stars: "El Potrero Chico Chiclets" campground offers stunning views and a social atmosphere, with basic amenities and tent or RV spots. Rates start around $5-10 USD per night.

Climbing Craving Comfort: Craving creature comforts? Opt for "Casa de Escalada La Poza," a climber-friendly guesthouse with dorms, private rooms, and even a swimming pool. Expect rates around $20-40 USD per night.

Hotels and Lodges: Several small hotels and lodges dot the town, offering basic amenities and local charm. Prices vary depending on amenities and season.

Dining Delights:

Local Treats: Hidalgo boasts several excellent restaurants serving traditional Mexican cuisine, from tacos and burritos to delicious grilled meats. Expect affordable prices and generous portions.

Climber Cafes: Fuel your ascents at climber-friendly cafes like "Casa Topo" or "El Potrero Chico Climbing Center." They offer coffee, smoothies, sandwiches, and even climbing gear rentals.

Self-Catering: Grocery stores and basic supermarkets stock up on essential supplies for camping or cooking in your accommodation.

Transportation in Town:

Walking: Hidalgo is a small town, easily walkable, allowing you to soak in the local atmosphere and stumble upon hidden gems.

Bikes and Taxis: Renting a bike offers freedom and exercise, while taxis are readily available for longer distances or transporting gear.

Tip: Hidalgo is a small town with limited ATMs. Bring enough cash for your stay, especially if you prefer local shops and restaurants.

MY Check

DATE _____

TOP 3 THINGS I LEARNT
_____
_____
_____

WHAT I AM WILLING TO TRY

THIS WEEK I FELT
_____

NEXT THING I WANT TO
_____
_____
_____

THINGS I ACCOMPLISHED THIS WEEK

WHAT WAS THE BEST THING ABOUT THE WEEK?

RATING
☆ ☆ ☆ ☆ ☆

El Potrero Chico

Chapter 2: Gearing Up for Success - Conquering Limestone with Confidence

El Potrero Chico beckons, but before you ascend its limestone heights, let's ensure you're equipped for victory. In this chapter, we'll explore the essential tools of your climbing trade, helping you navigate gear choices and maximize your comfort on the rock.

2.1: Packing Smart - Your Climbing Arsenal

Packing light is key, but don't skimp on the essentials. Here's a checklist for climbing success:

Harness: Your fortress on high! Choose a comfortable, well-fitting harness with enough loops for your gear. Consider renting initially before investing in your own.

Belay Device and Locking Carabiner: Your safety lifeline. Familiarize yourself with their use before hitting the cliffs. Most climbing camps offer renting options.

Climbing Shoes: Your trusty companions on the rock. Select snug-fitting shoes specific to your climbing style and skill level. Renting allows you to experiment before buying.

Helmet: Essential protection against falling rock and errant belay devices. Don't leave home without it!

Chalk Bag and Chalk: Keep your grip secure with climbing chalk and a handy bag to hold it. Refills are readily available at local shops.

Quickdraws: Clips connecting your rope to the bolts. Rent your first set until you understand your route needs.

Rope: The tether that binds you and your partner. Climbing camps usually offer rope rentals, ensuring the right length and thickness for your chosen routes.

Tip: Packing cubes keep your gear organized and easily accessible within your backpack.

2.2: Footwork Finesse - Choosing the Right Footwear

Your feet are your connection to the rock, so choosing the right footwear is crucial. Here's a breakdown:

Climbing Shoes: Aggressive downturned shoes are ideal for overhangs and technical climbs, while neutral shoes offer comfort for beginners and slab routes. Renting allows experimentation before buying.

Approach Shoes: Rugged footwear for the hike to the crag. Opt for breathable, supportive shoes with good traction. Consider trail runners if you plan on exploring beyond the climbs.

Comfortable Sandals: A must for post-climb relaxation and casual explorations around Hidalgo.

Tip: Break in your climbing shoes before your trip to avoid blisters and ensure proper fit.

2.3: Layering Up for Limestone Adventures

El Potrero Chico's weather can be unpredictable. Be prepared with flexible clothing options:

Sun Protection: Sunhat, sunglasses, and sunscreen are essential year-round. Pack SPF 50+ for exposed skin and lip balm for the Mexican sun.

Base Layer: Breathable fabric like wicking polyester wicks away sweat and keeps you cool.

Mid Layer: Pack a lightweight fleece or windbreaker for cooler mornings and changing weather.

Outer Layer: A versatile rain jacket or shell is invaluable for sudden downpours.

Climbing Pants: Opt for comfortable, flexible pants that allow for unrestricted movement. Consider convertible pants for added versatility.

Tip: Pack quick-drying clothing for efficient post-climb changes and minimal laundry needs.

2.4: Gearing Up for Multi-Pitch Adventures - Conquering Multi-Legged Giants

El Potrero Chico isn't just about single-pitch routes; it's a multi-pitch playground waiting to be explored. But tackling these longer ascents requires additional gear and planning. Let's ensure you're prepared for vertical marathons:

Haul Bag: Your mobile gear closet on the wall. Choose a comfortable, durable bag capable of carrying several sets of quickdraws, carabiners, slings, and snacks. Renting is an option for occasional multi-pitch ventures.

Rappelling Kit: Descend with confidence. Pack a rappel device (ATC or similar), rappel rings, and cord or webbing of appropriate length. Renting might be enough for beginners, but experienced climbers prefer their own gear.

Food and Water: Stay fueled and hydrated for extended climbs. Pack high-energy snacks like nuts, bars, and dried fruit. Bring a refillable water bottle and consider hydration bladders for easy access.

Extra Tips:

Helmet: Essential even more so on multi-pitch routes due to falling rock possibilities.

Headlamp: A must-have for late finishes or unexpected rappels in fading light.

First-aid kit: Be prepared for minor scrapes or injuries.

Sun protection: Reapply regularly, especially on longer climbs.

2.5: Climbing Etiquette and Leave No Trace Principles

The beauty of El Potrero Chico is a shared treasure. Let's ensure it remains pristine for generations to come by adhering to basic etiquette and Leave No Trace principles:

Climbing Etiquette:

Respect Others: Yield to climbers already on the route, give ample warning before starting your ascent, and be mindful of noise levels.

Communicate Clearly: Use clear belay commands and hand signals to ensure safety and avoid misunderstandings.

Pack It In, Pack It Out: Leave no trace of your presence at the crag. Take all trash, even cigarette butts, back to town for proper disposal.

Respect the Rock: Avoid unnecessary chalk markings or graffiti, and don't break holds or damage the climbing environment.

Offer Help: If you see someone struggling, offer assistance or advice respectfully. The climbing community thrives on shared knowledge and camaraderie.

Leave No Trace Principles:

Plan Ahead and Prepare: Research your chosen route, bring appropriate gear, and minimize your impact on the environment.

Travel and Camp on Durable Surfaces: Stick to established trails and designated campsites to avoid damaging fragile vegetation or sensitive areas.

Dispose of Waste Properly: Pack out all trash, including human waste, food scraps, and used toilet paper. Leave the crag cleaner than you found it.

Leave What You Find: Minimize altering the natural landscape. Avoid building structures, collecting plants or rocks, or disturbing wildlife.

Respect Wildlife: Give animals space and avoid feeding them. Store your food securely to prevent attracting unwanted guests.

Minimize Campfire Impacts: Use designated fire rings or stoves whenever possible.

Be Considerate of Other Visitors: Respect others' enjoyment of the crag by keeping noise levels to a minimum and being mindful of how your actions might affect them.

Every climber is responsible for protecting the magic of El Potrero Chico. By following these simple guidelines, we can ensure this limestone paradise thrives for generations to come.

In the next chapter, we'll delve deeper into the heart of this climbing wonderland. We'll explore the diverse crags, share insights on selecting the right routes for your skill level, and reveal some hidden gems waiting to be discovered. Get ready to map out your climbing adventure and prepare to be awestruck by the majesty of El Potrero Chico!

My Check

DATE _____

TOP 3 THINGS I LEARNT
_____
_____
_____

WHAT I AM WILLING TO TRY

THIS WEEK I FELT
_____

NEXT THING I WANT TO
_____
_____
_____

THINGS I ACCOMPLISHED THIS WEEK

WHAT WAS THE BEST THING ABOUT THE WEEK?

RATING
☆ ☆ ☆ ☆ ☆

Chapter 3: The Crags of El Potrero Chico

3.1: Charting Your Limestone Ascent - A Climber's Guide to the Major Sectors

El Potrero Chico, a symphony of limestone sculpted by wind and time, awaits your exploration. But with over 600 routes sprawled across 20 distinct sectors, where do you begin? Fear not, intrepid climber, for this chapter will be your trusty guide, offering route recommendations, safety tips, and pro insights for adventurers of all skill levels. So, lace up your climbing shoes, tighten your harness, and prepare to discover your perfect limestone melody within this grand amphitheater.

3.1.1 Peñaflor: The Crown Jewel - Big Walls and Iconic Classics (Latitude 25° 19' 22" N, Longitude 100° 10' 29" W)

A soaring wall adorned with legendary routes, Peñaflor is the Everest of El Potrero Chico. Here, multi-pitch epics like "Taj Mahal" and "Aztlán" beckon experienced climbers to test their endurance and technique on towering limestone canvases.

Recommendations:

- For the Elite: Tackle the infamous "Arathana" (5.13b), a masterpiece of sustained face climbing.
- Intermediate Odyssey: Embark on the multi-pitch adventure of "Space Boyz" (5.10c), offering spectacular views and challenging crux moves.
- Warm-Up Wall: Hone your skills on the single-pitch routes of "Los Pilares," perfect for a day of limestone indulgence.

Safety Tips:

- Multi-pitch climbing requires meticulous rope management, secure anchors, and clear communication.
- Be wary of loose rock during descents, especially on popular routes.
- Plan your ascents around the sun's path, seeking shade during the hottest hours.

Pro Insights:

Hire a local guide for your first multi-pitch adventure on Peñaflor. Their expertise will ensure safety and maximize your enjoyment.

Don't be intimidated by the big walls; Peñaflor offers shorter routes at various grades for climbers to test their mettle before tackling the giants.

Pack extra water and snacks, as multi-pitch ascents can take longer than anticipated.

3.1.2 El Toro: Single-Pitch Paradise - Slab, Overhang, and Technical Delights (Latitude 25° 19' 16" N, Longitude 100° 10' 49" W)

Sun-drenched walls and a plethora of single-pitch routes make El Toro a climber's haven. From technical overhangs like "Chinaco" (5.12d) to gentle slabs ideal for beginners, this sector offers something for everyone.

Recommendations:

Thrill Seekers: Conquer the fearsome "Chinaco," a steep endurance test with spectacular views.

Technical Delights: Challenge your footwork on "La Sombra" (5.11a), a technical masterpiece etched onto a smooth canvas.

Slab Sanctuary: Enjoy the gentle slopes and sunshine on "Los Pinos" (5.7), perfect for honing basic skills and soaking in the scenery.

Safety Tips:

Be mindful of falling rock on El Toro's steeper routes, especially during high activity periods.

Wear sunscreen and bring a hat; these sun-exposed walls offer minimal shade.

Watch out for crowds, especially at popular routes, and be courteous to other climbers.

Pro Insights:

El Toro is ideal for warming up or cooling down after tackling multi-pitch routes on Peñaflor.

Pack sticky rubber shoes for the technical routes, as the limestone's texture can be quite slick.

Explore the "El Cuervo" sector within El Toro for additional single-pitch options and a charming natural swimming pool.

3.1.3 La Silla: Beginner's Dream - Gentle Slopes and Sun-Drenched Rocks (Latitude 25° 19' 05" N, Longitude 100° 10' 26" W)

Basking in sunshine and offering gentle slopes, La Silla is the perfect launching pad for aspiring climbers. This sector's lower grades and approachable routes make it ideal for honing basic skills and building confidence.

Recommendations:

First Ascents: Start your limestone journey on "El Puente" (5.5), a fun slab route with easy belay access.

Building Confidence: Challenge yourself on "La Grieta" (5.7), a slightly steeper climb with a manageable crack feature.

Sunshine Sanctuary: Relax and enjoy the warm rock and panoramic views from "La Placa" (5.6), a perfect spot for picnics between climbs.

3.1.4 El Abra: Multi-Pitch Playground - Moderate Adventures and Stunning Views (Latitude 25° 19' 02" N, Longitude 100° 10' 13" W)

Craving multi-pitch adventures without tackling Peñaflor's intimidating wall? Look no further than El Abra, a sector offering moderate multi-pitch routes with breathtaking vistas across the canyon.

Recommendations:

Moderate Masterpiece: Embark on the classic "El Abra" (5.9), a multi-pitch journey with varied terrain and stunning views.

Technical Traverse: Test your footwork on "La Travesía" (5.10c), a multi-pitch adventure featuring exposed traverses and exciting rappels.

Warm-Up Wall: Hone your multi-pitch skills on the shorter routes of "El Peñón" (5.8), perfect for practicing rope management and communication.

Safety Tips:

While considered moderate, El Abra's routes still require proper multi-pitch techniques and safety precautions.

Be aware of loose rock on certain sections, especially after heavy rains.

Plan your ascents strategically to avoid the hottest midday hours, as some walls offer limited shade.

Pro Insights:

Hire a local guide for your first multi-pitch adventure in El Abra to ensure safety and maximize your enjoyment.

Pack extra water and snacks, as multi-pitch ascents can take longer than anticipated.

El Abra also offers single-pitch routes, including the popular "El Puente" (5.10b), ideal for advanced climbers looking for a quick technical challenge.

3.1.5 Otras Cumbres: Exploring Beyond the Main Areas - Hidden Gems and Unique Challenges (Latitude 25° 19' 22" N, Longitude 100° 10' 00" W)

Don't limit yourself to the main sectors! El Potrero Chico boasts several "Otras Cumbres" (other peaks) waiting to be explored. These hidden gems offer a diverse range of climbing experiences, from secluded cave routes to adventurous walks-offs.

Recommendations:

Cave Climbers: Delve into the subterranean world of "La Cueva de los Sueños" (5.11c), a challenging route requiring headlamp illumination.

Walking Off the Edge: Conquer the adrenaline-pumping "Valle de las Mulas" (5.10d), a multi-pitch adventure culminating in a thrilling walk-off descent.

Technical Playground: Challenge your footwork on the crimpy face climbs of "Las Chivas" (5.12a), an isolated sector offering stunning views and demanding routes.

Safety Tips:

Research your chosen route thoroughly, as information may be limited for "Otras Cumbres."

Download offline maps and GPS coordinates to avoid getting lost in the maze of sectors.

Consider hiring a local guide with expertise in the specific area you want to explore.

Pro Insights:

"Otras Cumbres" is ideal for experienced climbers seeking unique challenges and a sense of adventure.

Be prepared for longer hikes to reach certain sectors, and pack accordingly with plenty of water and snacks.

Leave no trace in these less-traveled areas; respect the environment and minimize your impact.

3.2: Navigating the Limestone Maze - Selecting Routes for Your Skill Level

El Potrero Chico's abundance can be overwhelming. How do you choose the right climb for your skill level and aspirations? Fear not, climber, for this section unravels the mysteries of grading systems and offers recommendations to ensure your ascents are both achievable and exhilarating.

Demystifying the Grades:

Climbing difficulty varies globally, but El Potrero Chico primarily uses the Yosemite Decimal System (YDS). This system ranges from 5.0 (easiest) to 5.15 (hardest), with subdivisions (a, b, c, d) indicating increasing difficulty within each grade. Additional letters (r, x) signify routes with specific challenges like runouts or dangerous falls.

Beyond the Numbers:

Grading is just one factor to consider. Remember:

Route style: Overhangs, slabs, cracks, and technical face climbs demand different skills and strengths. Choose routes that complement your climbing style.

Reading beta: "Beta" refers to tips and advice on climbing a specific route. Research your chosen route online or in guidebooks to understand its cruxes, potential hazards, and essential movements.

Partner dynamics: Climb with someone whose skill level and temperament match yours. Communication and trust are crucial on the rock.

Honest self-assessment: Don't push your limits blindly. Choose routes that challenge you, but are achievable with your current skillset. Overconfidence can lead to accidents.

Recommendations by Skill Level:

Beginners (5.5 - 5.7): Start on gentle slopes and slab routes in La Silla or El Toro. Work on basic skills like footwork, balance, and belaying. Seek guidance from experienced climbers or consider hiring a guide.

Intermediate (5.8 - 5.10): Explore the moderate multi-pitch routes of El Abra or tackle single-pitch challenges in El Toro. Build endurance and improve technique on varied terrain.

Advanced (5.11+): Conquer the technical masterpieces of Peñaflor or challenge your endurance on multi-pitch adventures in El Abra or other "Otras Cumbres" sectors. Be prepared for demanding physical and mental challenges.

3.3: Deciphering the Limestone Secrets - Finding Beta and Topo Maps

So, you've chosen your dream route. Now, how do you decipher its intricacies and plan your ascent? Enter the world of beta and topo maps, your essential tools for unlocking the secrets of the rock.

Online Resources:

- 8a.nu: An extensive online database with route descriptions, photos, user beta, and topo maps for El Potrero Chico.
- The Big Wall Project: Features detailed multi-pitch route descriptions, including topo maps, anchor locations, and climbing strategies.
- Mountain Project: Offers user-generated content, including route beta, photos, and discussions on specific climbs.

Other Guidebooks:

- "El Potrero Chico Climbing Guide" by John Long: A comprehensive guidebook with detailed route descriptions, topo maps, and historical information.

- "Mexican Climbing" by Chris Sharma: Features stunning photography and beta insights from legendary climber Chris Sharma.
- Local guidebooks: Available in Hidalgo at climbing shops and cafes, often with specific information on recent route updates and conditions.

Local Knowledge:

Climbing shops and cafes: Talk to seasoned climbers and guides at local businesses. They often have firsthand knowledge of current conditions, beta insights, and recommendations.

Fellow climbers: Connect with other climbers at the crag who might have climbed your chosen route recently and can offer valuable tips and tricks.

Remember: Be responsible with beta. Don't rely solely on online information; always verify crucial details like anchor locations and potential hazards with guidebooks or local experts.

My Check

DATE _____

TOP 3 THINGS I LEARNT
_____
_____
_____

THIS WEEK I FELT
_____

NEXT THING I WANT TO
_____
_____
_____

WHAT I AM WILLING TO TRY

THINGS I ACCOMPLISHED THIS WEEK

WHAT WAS THE BEST THING ABOUT THE WEEK?

RATING
☆ ☆ ☆ ☆ ☆

Chapter 4: Mastering the Climb - Unveiling the Secrets of Limestone Ascension

With your route chosen, beta gleaned, and gear at the ready, it's time to face the limestone. In this chapter, we'll delve into the heart of climbing, exploring essential techniques, safety protocols, and tips to maximize your enjoyment and success on the rock.

4.1: Warming Up for Success - Movement Techniques for Confidence and Efficiency

Starting cold on a climb is a recipe for disaster. Embrace the warming-up ritual:

Dynamic stretches: Gentle movements like leg swings, arm circles, and jumping jacks increase blood flow and prepare your muscles for exertion.

Static stretches: Hold stretches for 15-30 seconds on major muscle groups like hamstrings, calves, and shoulders, improving flexibility and range of motion.

Easy climbing: Start with low-grade routes or easier sections of your chosen climb to warm up your fingers and build confidence.

Movement Fundamentals:

Body positioning: Find your center of gravity, engage your core, and maintain a balanced posture for efficient movement.

Footwork: Learn how to use your feet for stability, power, and precision. Master edging, smearing, and heel-hooking techniques specific to limestone climbing.

Handholds: Grip holds firmly, engage your fingers and muscles efficiently, and learn to transition smoothly between different hold types.

Reading the rock: Analyze the route, anticipate your next moves, and use the rock features to your advantage.

Pro Tip: Take breaks during your climb, shake out your arms, and drink water to maintain energy and focus.

4.2: Dancing on Limestone - Footwork Secrets for Edging and Slabs

Limestone climbing demands precise footwork. Here's how to master the dance:

Edging: Hone the art of using small holds with confidence. Trust your feet, engage your core, and maintain balance even on tiny edges.

Smearing: Embrace the friction! Learn to use the entire surface of your shoes to grip smooth slabs and sloping rock.

Heel-hooking: Unlock an extra gear by engaging your heel against ledges or pockets for additional stability and power.

Slab Techniques:

Micro-movements: Master tiny adjustments of your feet and body position to maintain balance on even the most delicate slabs.

Friction dancing: Use your full body weight to generate friction and stay glued to the rock.

Mental game: Trust your feet, stay calm, and focus on each movement with laser precision.

Pro Tip: Practice footwork drills on the ground before taking them to the wall. Visualize successful climbs and build confidence in your abilities.

4.3: The Language of the Rope - Belaying and Rappelling Fundamentals

Safety is paramount in climbing. Mastering belaying and rappelling techniques is crucial:

Belaying:

Know your gear: Familiarize yourself with your belay device, locking carabiner, and rope management techniques.

Communication: Establish clear hand signals and verbal cues with your climbing partner.

Smoothness: Pay attention to the climber, take up slack smoothly, and provide a controlled fall if necessary.

Rappelling:

Anchor setup: Learn how to build secure anchors using slings, carabiners, and appropriate knots.

Rope management: Double-check your rappelling setup, ensure proper rope threading through your device, and avoid friction buildup.

Descent technique: Lean back, control your speed using the brake line, and communicate clearly with your belayer during the descent.

Pro Tip: Practice belaying and rappelling under the supervision of an experienced climber or take a dedicated course to ensure proper technique and safety awareness.

4.4: Conquering the Vertical Marathon - Multi-Pitch Strategy for Success

El Potrero Chico's multi-pitch routes offer epic journeys, but traversing these limestone walls requires meticulous planning and strategic execution. Let's delve into rope management, anchor systems, and teamwork tactics to ensure your multi-pitch adventure is both safe and exhilarating.

Rope Management:

Minimize friction: Use double ropes to avoid rope drag and keep the system running smoothly.

Communication is key: Clearly signal when switching leads, belaying, and lowering the climber.

Organize your gear: Keep slings, carabiners, and quickdraws readily accessible within reach.

Anchor Systems:

Learn the basics: Master building secure anchors using slings, carabiners, and appropriate knots like the double fisherman's bend.

Adapt to the situation: Choose anchor configurations based on the terrain, rock quality, and number of climbers.

Double-check everything: Before rappelling or lowering your partner, meticulously inspect your anchor for security and redundancy.

Teamwork Makes the Dream Work:

Clear communication: Establish roles, hand signals, and verbal cues beforehand to avoid confusion and misunderstandings on the wall.

Trust and support: Rely on your partner, offer encouragement, and be prepared to assist with technical challenges or unexpected situations.

Shared responsibility: Both team members should be familiar with anchor building, rope management, and basic rescue techniques.

Pro Tip: Consider hiring a local guide for your first multi-pitch adventure in El Potrero Chico. Their expertise will ensure safety and maximize your enjoyment.

4.5: Climbing Through Your Mind - Conquering the Mental Game and Embracing the Journey

Climbing isn't just about physical prowess; it's a mental dance. Here's how to navigate the inner terrain and enjoy every step of your limestone ascent:

Staying Focused:

Visualization: Mentally rehearse your moves, imagine success, and build confidence before attempting challenging sections.

Deep breathing: Control your breath, calm your nerves, and maintain focus even in demanding situations.

Positive self-talk: Encourage yourself, celebrate small victories, and overcome negative thoughts that might hold you back.

Pushing Your Limits:

Step outside your comfort zone: Gradually challenge yourself with harder routes, but be smart and listen to your body.

Embrace failure: View falls as learning opportunities, analyze mistakes, and come back stronger.

Seek inspiration: Watch other climbers, learn from their techniques, and draw motivation from their achievements.

Enjoying the Ride:

Be present: Savor the moment, appreciate the stunning views, and feel the connection with the rock beneath your fingertips.

Celebrate successes: Big or small, acknowledge your accomplishments and give yourself a pat on the back for every conquered challenge.

Share the experience: Connect with fellow climbers, build friendships, and enjoy the camaraderie that thrives in this unique community.

Pro Tip: Remember, climbing is a journey, not a destination. Focus on the process, be kind to yourself, and allow yourself to experience the pure joy of movement and connection with the vertical world.

So, lace up your shoes, embrace the challenge, and climb on!

Chapter 5: Beyond the Climb - Embracing the Full El Potrero Chico Experience

Your fingers may be raw, your muscles may ache, but your heart is full. El Potrero Chico has cast its spell, and the limestone symphony resonates within you. But there's more to this Mexican paradise than just vertical adventures. Let's explore the world beyond the crag and discover the tapestry of culture, community, and hidden gems that await you.

5.1: Rest and Recovery - Refueling Your Engine for Future Ascents

Climbing demands physical and mental resilience. Here's how to nurture your body and mind for further exploits:

Active Regeneration: Gentle movement like yoga, swimming, or hiking aids recovery and keeps your blood flowing.

Stretching: Dedicate time to static stretches focusing on your major muscle groups to improve flexibility and range of motion.

Hydration: Replenish lost fluids and electrolytes with plenty of water and consider sports drinks for enhanced recovery.

Rest and Nourishment: Allow your body adequate rest, prioritize sleep, and fuel your muscles with healthy, protein-rich food.

Pro Tip: Treat yourself to a massage in Hidalgo! Professional therapists can work out climbing-specific muscle tension and leave you feeling rejuvenated.

5.2: El Potrero Chico Beyond the Crag - Unearthing Cultural Treasures and Local Delights

Hidalgo and its surrounding region offer a wealth of experiences beyond the limestone walls:

Cultural Immersion: Explore the charming town of Hidalgo, visit the historic church, browse local crafts, and soak up the Mexican atmosphere.

Day Trips to Magical Pueblos: Embark on adventures to nearby "Pueblos Mágicos" like Real de Catorce, a ghost town steeped in silver mining history, or Xilitla, a surrealist paradise designed by Edward James.

Nature's Embrace: Hike through canyons, swim in natural pools, or explore the nearby Sierra de Cardonal National Park for breath-taking mountain views and diverse flora and fauna.

Culinary Delights: Dive into the world of Mexican cuisine from traditional tacos and mole to fresh seafood and local specialties. Be adventurous and try new flavors!

Pro Tip: Learn a few basic Spanish phrases to enhance your interactions with locals and enrich your cultural experience.

5.3: Climbing Camaraderie - Sharing the Stoke and Building Connections

The climbing community in El Potrero Chico is vibrant and welcoming. Dive in and embrace the following:

Joining Group Climbs: Connect with other climbers at the crag or through social media groups and join their adventures.

Sharing Knowledge and Beta: Offer insights and advice to newer climbers and learn from more experienced ones. The climbing community thrives on mutual support and knowledge sharing.

Celebratory Gatherings: Join climbers for post-climb dinners, share stories, and forge lasting friendships around the shared passion for limestone ascents.

Pro Tip: Respect climber etiquette at the crag, be mindful of others, and contribute to a positive and inclusive community atmosphere.

5.4: Climbing with a Conscience - Sustainable Practices for a Lasting Limestone Legacy

El Potrero Chico's beauty is unparalleled, but it's our responsibility to preserve it for future generations. Here's how to minimize your impact and climb with a sustainable mindset:

Leave No Trace: Pack out all trash, including toilet paper and biodegradable wipes. Utilize designated waste bins or carry a personal bag.

Minimize Chalk Use: Stick to designated chalk zones, use liquid chalk sparingly, and avoid over-chalking on the rock. Excessive chalk build-up can damage the rock and affect its friction characteristics.

Respect Vegetation: Stay on established trails, avoid disturbing plant life, and camp only in designated areas.

Water Conservation: Pack a reusable water bottle and refill it at designated areas to minimize single-use plastics.

Minimize Noise and Light Pollution: Respect climbers and locals by keeping noise levels down, especially in the evenings. Use headlamps responsibly and avoid disturbing wildlife.

Pro Tip: Support local conservation efforts by donating to organizations working to protect El Potrero Chico and its fragile ecosystem.

MY Check

DATE _____

TOP 3 THINGS I LEARNT
_____
_____
_____

THIS WEEK I FELT
_____

NEXT THING I WANT TO
_____
_____
_____

WHAT I AM WILLING TO TRY

THINGS I ACCOMPLISHED THIS WEEK

WHAT WAS THE BEST THING ABOUT THE WEEK?

RATING
☆ ☆ ☆ ☆ ☆

El Potrero Chico

Appendix: Climbing El Potrero Chico with Confidence

A. Deepening Your Journey - Resources and Further Information

As your love for El Potrero Chico grows, you'll crave more knowledge and opportunities for connection. Here are some valuable resources to keep you climbing:

Websites:

- Climb Potrero Mountain Guides: https://potrerochico.org/
- 8a.nu: https://www.8a.nu/
- The Big Wall Project: https://www.thebigwall.org/
- Mountain Project: https://www.mountainproject.com/

Magazines:

- Rock & Ice: https://www.facebook.com/rockandice/
- Climbing Magazine: https://www.climbing.com/

- Gripped Climbing Magazine: https://gripped.com/

Climbing Schools:

- Climb Potrero Mountain Guides: https://potrerochico.org/
- El Potrero Chico Guides: https://www.elpotrerochicoguides.com/
- Mexican Climbing: https://pjammcycling.com/zone/212.Mexico-Top-Bike-Climbs

Pro Tip: Engage with online forums and communities to connect with climbers, share experiences, and learn from seasoned veterans.

B. Conversion Tables

International Climbing Grade Conversion Charts: https://www.mec.ca/en/explore/climbing-grade-conversion

Grades and Grade Conversions: https://www.thecrag.com/en/article/gradesonthecrag

Rockfax Grade Conversions: https://rockfax.com/news/2020/03/11/rockfax-grade-tables-updated/

8a.nu El Potrero Chico Topo and Route Descriptions: https://www.mountainproject.com/map/105910764/el-potrero-chico

These resources offer comprehensive conversion tables for *various climbing grading systems, including YDS (Yosemite Decimal System) commonly used in El Potrero Chico. You can compare your familiar grade system with the YDS grades found in El Potrero Chico route descriptions.*

C. Sample Packing List for El Potrero Chico:
Climbing Gear:

Harness: Choose a comfortable and well-fitting harness with gear loops for your climbing accessories.

Belay device: Ensure you're familiar with a standard belay device like an ATC guide or Grigri.

Locking carabiners: Pack 2-3 locking carabiners for belaying, rappelling, and anchor construction.

Non-locking carabiners: Several non-locking carabiners for clipping into quickdraws and gear slings.

Quickdraws: 8-12 quickdraws depending on the length of your chosen routes.

Rope: Select a climbing rope of appropriate length and diameter for your intended routes.

Helmet: Protect your head from falling rock and rappelling mishaps.

Climbing shoes: Choose comfortable and well-fitting climbing shoes suited to the limestone climbing style of El Potrero Chico.

Chalk bag and chalk: Bring enough chalk for your sessions and consider refillable options for sustainability.

Clothing:

T-shirts and tank tops: Breathable and quick-drying options for hot weather.

Climbing pants or shorts: Durable and comfortable for movement on the rock.

Sports bra (for women): Supportive and comfortable for physical activity.

Light jacket or fleece: For early mornings or cooler evenings.

Sun hat and sunglasses: Protect yourself from the sun's harsh rays.

Hiking boots or approach shoes: Comfortable footwear for reaching the crags and hiking trails.

Other Essentials:

Backpack: A comfortable and functional backpack to carry your gear to the crag.

Water bottle or hydration pack: Stay hydrated throughout your climbing sessions.

Sunscreen and insect repellent: Protect yourself from the sun and potential insects.

Headlamp: For climbing in the shade or rappelling after dark.

First-aid kit: Be prepared for minor injuries.

Snacks and food: Pack high-energy snacks and light meals for your climbing days.

Cash and local currency: Some shops and cafes may not accept cards.

Spanish phrasebook (optional): Can be helpful for basic communication.

Additional Items (Optional):

Crash pad: If you plan to try bouldering or top-rope soloing.

Finger tape: Protect your fingertips from blisters.

Camera: Capture your El Potrero Chico adventure memories.

Music and speakers: Enjoy tunes while relaxing at the crag (use responsibly and be mindful of others).

Bonus Section

6.1: Glossary of Climbing Terms

This comprehensive list provides definitions for beginner and experienced climbers alike, allowing everyone to navigate the jargon of the vertical world!

Basic Terms:

Anchor: A secure system of ropes, slings, and carabiners used to belay, rappel, and manage falls.

Belay: The act of securing a climber with a belay device and rope while they ascend.

Carabiner: A metal clip with a gate used for connecting ropes, slings, and gear to anchors and climbing systems.

Chalk: Powder used to improve grip on the rock by absorbing moisture from your hands.

Crampon: A metal device with points attached to boots for increased traction on ice and snow.

Gear loops: Loops on a harness for carrying climbing equipment like quickdraws, slings, and carabiners.

Harness: A supportive piece of equipment worn around the hips and legs to secure the climber during falls.

Helmet: Protects the head from falling rock and rappelling mishaps.

Quickdraw: Two carabiners connected by a short sling used for clipping into bolts on routes.

Rappelling: Descending a cliff face using a rope and belay device.

Rope: A long, strong cord used for belaying, rappelling, and managing falls.

Sling: A looped length of webbing used for building anchors, attaching gear, and extending reach.

Climbing Techniques:

Crimping: Holding onto small edges with the tips of your fingers.

Edging: Using the outside edge of your foot for precise footwork on small holds.

Face climbing: Climbing on vertical or slightly overhanging terrain using hand and footholds.

Heel-hooking: Using your heel against ledges or pockets for additional stability and power.

Jamming: Pushing hands or fingers into cracks in the rock for secure holds.

Mantling: Using your arms and legs to push yourself onto a higher ledge.

Smearing: Using the entire surface of your shoes to grip smooth slabs and sloping rock.

Traversing: Moving laterally across the rock face.

Climbing Grades:

Yosemite Decimal System (YDS): The most common grading system in North America, ranging from 5.0 (easiest) to 5.15 (hardest) with subdivisions (a, b, c, d) indicating increasing difficulty within each grade.

French grading: Often used in Europe, ranging from 1 (easiest) to 9c+ (hardest).

British grading: Used in the UK, ranging from VD (Very Difficult) to E11 (extreme).

Other Terms:

Beta: Advice or tips on climbing a specific route.

Bouldering: Climbing short, difficult routes without ropes or harnesses, usually close to the ground.

Flash: First attempt to climb a route.

Lead climbing: Climbing with the rope attached to your harness, placing protection as you ascend.

Multi-pitch climbing: Climbing routes longer than a single rope length, requiring rappelling between sections.

Onsight: Climbing a route without any prior knowledge or beta.

Project: A route that a climber is working on to perfect and eventually send.

Redpoint: Climbing a route after having previously fallen on it.

Send: Successfully completing a climb.

Top-roping: Climbing a route with the rope already pre-fixed at the top, eliminating the need for lead climbing and placing protection.

6.2: Useful Phrases and Numbers with Pronunciation Guide (Spanish - English):

Phrases:

Hello: Hola (OH-lah)

Goodbye: Adiós (ah-dee-OHS)

Please: Por favor (por fah-VOR)

Thank you: Gracias (GRA-see-ahs)

You're welcome: De nada (deh NAH-dah)

Excuse me: Disculpe (dees-kool-PEH)

Do you speak English? ¿Habla inglés? (AH-blah een-GLES)

Yes: Sí (see)

No: No (noh)

Water: Agua (AH-gwah)

Food: Comida (coh-MEE-dah)

Bathroom: Baño (BAN-yo)

Help: Ayuda (eye-OO-dah)

Hospital: Hospital (oh-speet-AHL)

Numbers:

1: Uno (OO-no)

2: Dos (dohs)

3: Tres (tres)

4: Cuatro (KWA-tro)

5: Cinco (SIN-co)

6: Seis (says)

7: Siete (SYE-teh)

8: Ocho (OH-cho)

9: Nueve (NWEH-veh)

10: Diez (dyes)

11: Once (OHN-say)

12: Doce (DOH-seh)

13: Trece (treh-seh)

14: Catorce (kah-TOR-seh)

15: Quince (KEEN-seh)

16: Dieciséis (dyays-ee-SAY-ees)

17: Diecisiete (dyays-ee-see-YEH-teh)

18: Dieciocho (dyays-ee-oh-CHO)

19: Diecinueve (dyays-ee-eh-NWEH-veh)

20: Veinte (vayn-teh)

Additional Phrases:

Where is the nearest restaurant? ¿Dónde está el restaurante más cercano? (DON-deh es-TAH el res-tau-RAHNT meh-yas ser-KAH-no)

Can I have the bill, please? La cuenta, por favor. (lah KWEHN-tah, por fah-VOR)

How much is it? ¿Cuánto cuesta? (KWAN-toh KWEHS-tah)

Do you accept credit cards? ¿Aceptan tarjetas de crédito? (ah-sep-TAN tar-HEH-tas deh KREH-dee-toh)

I don't understand. No entiendo. (noh en-TYEN-do)

Could you please repeat that? ¿Puede repetir eso, por favor? (¿PWEH-deh reh-peh-TEER eh-soh, por fah-VOR?)

Nice to meet you! Encantado de conocerte. (en-kan-TAH-do deh koh-no-SER-teh)

Good luck! ¡Buena suerte! (BWEH-nah SWEHR-teh)

Have fun! ¡Diviértete! (dee-vyair-TYEH-teh)

Remember, pronunciation can vary depending on the region, so don't be afraid to adjust your tone and intonation to communicate effectively. Most importantly, have fun practicing your Spanish and using these phrases during your El Potrero Chico adventure!

6.3 Downloadable Maps and Recommended Climbing Areas

Downloadable Maps and Recommended Climbing Areas for El Potrero Chico:

Maps:

8a.nu El Potrero Chico Topo: https://www.8a.nu/crags/sportclimbing/spain/l-olla/

- This comprehensive online topo provides detailed information on routes, sectors, and anchor locations. You can download a PDF version for offline use.

Climb Potrero Mountain Guides Map: https://potrerochico.org/about/this-website

- This downloadable PDF map from Climb Potrero Mountain Guides gives an overview of the climbing sectors and approach trails.

Google Maps: Download the offline map of El Potrero Chico within the Google Maps app for basic navigation and access to nearby amenities.

Recommended Climbing Areas:

La Plaza: Great for beginners and intermediate climbers with moderate routes and slabs. Easy access from the village.

El Toro: Offers a variety of routes for all skill levels, from beginner slabs to challenging overhangs.

El Abra: Home to numerous multi-pitch routes, providing epic adventure climbs with stunning views.

Peñaflor: Renowned for its technical face climbs and challenging overhangs, suitable for experienced climbers.

Otras Cumbres: Explores lesser-known sectors beyond the main walls, offering diverse terrain and a more secluded climbing experience.

Beyond the Climb: 10 Must-Do Activities

Explore the Magical Town of Hidalgo: Take a stroll through the charming cobblestone streets of Hidalgo, visit the historic Church of San Miguel Arcángel, browse the local crafts market, and soak up the authentic Mexican atmosphere.

Day Trip to Real de Catorce: Embark on an adventure to Real de Catorce, a ghost town steeped in silver mining history. Explore the abandoned mines, wander through the eerie streets, and marvel at the majestic desert landscapes.

Discover the Surrealist Paradise of Xilitla: Immerse yourself in the whimsical world of Edward James' surrealist garden Las Pozas. Explore bizarre sculptures, wander through secret paths, and swim in cascading waterfalls hidden within the lush jungle.

Hike and Swim in the Sierra de Cardonal National Park: Escape the heat and immerse yourself in nature by hiking through the scenic trails of the Sierra de Cardonal National

Park. Spot diverse flora and fauna, enjoy breathtaking views, and take a refreshing dip in the natural pools.

Indulge in Local Delights: Savor the rich flavors of Mexican cuisine by trying traditional dishes like tacos, mole, fresh seafood, and regional specialties. Don't miss out on sampling local delicacies like cabrito (roasted goat) and nopales (cactus) dishes.

Learn Spanish and Connect with Locals: Pick up a few basic Spanish phrases to enhance your interactions with locals, learn about their culture, and create lasting connections. Consider taking a Spanish language class or hiring a local guide for deeper cultural immersion.

Explore Gruta de Garcia Caves: Discover the wonders of the subterranean world by joining a guided tour through the Gruta de Garcia Caves. Marvel at the impressive stalactites and stalagmites, wander through ancient chambers, and experience the breathtaking beauty of this natural wonder.

Relax and Rejuvenate: After a day of climbing and exploring, unwind and pamper yourself with a relaxing massage or spa treatment. Several local businesses offer therapeutic massages tailored to climbers' needs, helping you recover and get ready for your next adventure.

Attend a Traditional Fiesta: Immerse yourself in the festive spirit of a Mexican fiesta by joining in the vibrant celebrations that often take place throughout the year. Dance to lively music, savor delicious food, and experience the warm hospitality of the local community.

Stargaze Under the Magical Sky: Escape the light pollution and gaze at the awe-inspiring night sky above El Potrero Chico. With minimal light interference, you can witness a dazzling display of stars, planets, and even the Milky Way galaxy, making it a truly unforgettable experience.

Printed in the USA
CPSIA information can be obtained
at www.ICGtesting.com
LVHW021645211124
797256LV00009B/372